Garden Desig
Beginners

Step-by-Step Comprehensive Guide on How to Design Your Garden to Have the Much-Needed Appeal and Functionality

Introduction

If you had told me I would be as big on gardening as I am today five years ago, I would have probably laughed in your face. Not because I found the idea of gardening abhorring or tedious; not at all, that's for sure. The reason was that I didn't have the time, and, to be brutally honest, I didn't even know how to get started. I have always enjoyed watching YouTube videos of famous gardeners. However, I had no clue that binge-watching my favorite YouTube gardening channel would plunge me deep into a lifelong gardening journey that would fill my days with so much joy.

Getting Me Started

Are you curious to know how I got started? Well, I got my feet wet on gardening during the Covid era. Being cooped up indoors all day was taking a toll on me. The need for something to occupy my mind and the desire to grow food to provide for my family during those hard times made me interested in gardening. What is more, I actually had the space and time. I started small with a few veggies and eventually got my hands dirty with bigger projects (think growing an entire year's produce, etc.) Today, I can confidently say gardening has always been a lifelong fulfillment waiting to happen. I can feed my family, share with my local community, have more to sell, and make a decent living while doing what I love.

But my gardening endeavors went well beyond the need for self-sustenance. I also badly wanted to spruce up my yard. Since I couldn't visit all (or any) of my favorite places during COVID-19, I had to create something comforting and aesthetically pleasing... somewhere I could really unwind in, especially after a long day of numerous Zoom meetings. And, ladies and gentlemen, that's how I got hooked (and, frankly, got really good) at gardening.

Getting You Started

If you are thinking of creating such a space in your home, then look no further than this guide. All you need, apart from the knowledge in these pages, are the right tools, plants, and a few other things, all of which I will gladly guide you through.

I'm no expert. Far from it. But then again, who really is in this field? I have my fair share of bad seasons in the garden. But from my years of chopping, changing, and practicing endlessly, I've learned more than enough to guide you on your gardening journey. In fact, I will even go so far as to say that my main selling point as to why this is the right guide for you is that I have already made a thousand missteps that I will gladly help you steer clear of.

I have painstakingly curated this book to fully serve you as a gardener, regardless of your skill level, so you're able to design your home's ideal landscape. I'm also humble enough to admit that my aim for writing this book is twofold – to educate you and to learn along the way as well.

Let's do this!

PS: I'd like your feedback. If you are happy with this book, please leave a review on Amazon.

Please leave a review for this book on Amazon by visiting the page below:

https://amzn.to/2VMR5qr

Table of Contents

Introduction **2**

Chapter 1: Understanding the Basics of Garden Design – A Comprehensive Exploration **8**

    Elements of Garden Design 8

    Types of Garden Styles 19

Chapter 2: Planning Your Garden – A Step-by-Step Guide **33**

    Part I: Setting Your Goals 33

    Part II: Assessing Your Space 38

    Part III: Climate and Soil Considerations 44

Chapter 3: Creating a Garden Layout **50**

    A) Drawing a Basic Layout 50

    B) Zoning Your Garden 57

C) Designing Pathways and Structures 61

Chapter 4: Incorporating Functional Elements in Your Garden 73

A) Seating Areas and Patios 73

B) Water Features 83

C) Garden Lighting 93

Chapter 5: Soil Preparation and Planting – A Comprehensive Guide 105

A) Soil Testing and Improvement 105

B) Planting Techniques 112

C) Mulching and Watering 119

Chapter 6: Constructing Garden Features – A Comprehensive Guide 127

A) Building Raised Beds 127

B) Installing Pathways 133

C) Setting Up Garden Structures (Pergolas, Arbors) 139

Conclusion **147**

Reference **149**

Chapter 1: Understanding the Basics of Garden Design – A Comprehensive Exploration

In this chapter, we will comprehensively cover the basics of garden design. Getting familiar with these basics will provide you with a solid foundation that will be crucial in helping you create the garden of your dreams. Understanding these fundamentals is crucial for anyone who wants to design a garden effectively. It will, among other things, ensure you make informed decisions and avoid common gardening design pitfalls. This chapter will equip you with the essential knowledge and principles that you need to do this gardening design thing like a pro right off the jump.

Let's get started.

Elements of Garden Design

The garden design combines three major elements: ***aesthetics, functionality, and horticulture***. When all three come together perfectly, the result is a beautiful and practical outdoor space. Regardless of your present status in the gardening design world – whether you have some experience to fall back on or are a complete novice – having a thorough understanding of the primary elements of garden design can (and most certainly will) help you create a garden that is both cohesive and inviting.

Important note: Elements of garden design are also commonly referred to as *"principles."* They are one and the same.

Here are the key elements to consider:

- **Unity and Harmony**

Unity, as far as garden design goes, refers to the *consistent use of design elements to create a cohesive look*. This can be achieved through repetition of plants, colors, textures, and materials. On the other hand, **harmony** ensures that all parts of the garden actually *work together to create a pleasing whole*.

Three main elements help actualize unity and harmony:

1. *Repetition*:

Refers to repeating elements such as plant types, colors, or materials throughout the garden.

2. Consistency:

Refers to using a consistent style, such as a formal or informal style, to unify the space. We'll comprehensively explore styles in the final section of the chapter.

3. Themes:

This refers to adopting a consistent theme, with examples of *tropical, cottage, or modern*, to guide your plant and material choices.

- **Balance**

Balance in a garden can either be **symmetrical or asymmetrical**. Symmetrical balance points to mirroring elements on both sides of the central axis to create a formal look. Asymmetrical balance, which is more informal, uses different elements to create an overall sense of balance.

Let's briefly touch on both to enhance your understanding:

1. *Symmetrical Balance:* This one is often seen in formal gardens and involves creating mirror images on either side of a central point.

2. *Asymmetrical Balance*: This is achieved through carefully placing different elements to achieve visual equilibrium.

- **Scale and Proportion**

Scale and proportion ensure that the elements of your garden are in harmony with each other and with the garden as a whole. This includes the size of plants, garden furniture, and other structures related to each other and the space.

Here is a brief word on both:

1. *Scale*: Scale refers to the *size of elements in relation to each other*. For example, large sculptures or structures in a small garden can overwhelm the space.

2. *Proportion*: This one involves the *relationship between the elements and the overall space*. For example, a large tree should not overshadow a small garden bed.

- **Color**

Color is one of the most noticeable elements of garden design and can evoke different emotions, not to mention set various moods. Colors can be warm (reds, yellows, oranges) or cool (blues, greens, purples) and can be used to create depth, highlight features, or draw attention.

There are two main elements with this one:

1. *Color Schemes*: There is an array of schemes to choose from, with examples of *monochromatic* (one color), *analogous* (colors next to each other on the color wheel), *complementary* (colors opposite on the color wheel), or *triadic* (three colors evenly spaced on the color wheel).

2. *Seasonal Color*: This one involves planning for different colors throughout the seasons. For instance, you may consider planning for plants that bloom in different seasons to ensure year-round color.

- **Texture**

Texture in a garden comes from the surfaces of plants and hardscapes, as well as other garden features. Texture adds *interest* and *contrast* and helps create depth and richness in your garden design.

There are two main elements to consider:

1. *Plant Texture*: The foliage you choose can be *fine* (delicate leaves), *medium* (average-sized leaves), or *coarse* (large, bold leaves).

2. *Hardscape Texture:* With this one, you need to carefully consider the surfaces of paths, walls, and other structures, as they all contribute to the overall aesthetic of the garden.

- **Line**

Lines in a garden design guide the eye and direct movement. They can be created by the edge of a path, a row of plants, or the outline of a flower bed.

There are two main kinds of lines:

1. *Straight Lines*: These are often used in formal gardens, primarily to help create a sense of order and direction.

2. *Curved Lines*: These provide a more relaxed, natural feel, and they can make a small space seem larger. They are often used in informal or naturalistic gardens.

- **Form**

Form is the shape and structure of garden objects, including plants, garden beds, and hardscapes. The form of a plant can be *upright, spreading, weeping, or mounding*.

There are two main elements to consider:

1. *Plant Forms:*

Image showing plant form

Trees, shrubs, perennials, and annuals all have distinct forms that contribute to the garden's overall design.

2. *Structural Forms:*

Elements like arches, pergolas, and sculptures add form to the garden.

- **Light**

Light influences the garden's appearance at different times of the day and year. It also affects plant growth and the overall mood of the garden.

You have two main options to consider:

1. *Natural Light*: Understanding how sunlight moves across your garden will help you in planning your plant placement.
2. *Artificial Lighting*: You can use this to extend enjoyment of the garden into the evening. You can also use it to highlight features.

- **Rhythm and Movement**

Rhythm and movement guide the eye through the garden and help create a sense of flow. This can be achieved through two aspects: the repetition of elements and the strategic placement of features:

1. *Repetition*: With this one, you can consider using repeated elements, such as plant clusters, paving patterns, or colors, to create a sense of rhythm.

2. *Transition*: Incorporating smooth and gradual changes in plant height, color, and texture will help guide the eye smoothly through the garden and make it more aesthetic.

- **Contrast**

Contrast adds visual interest. It also helps highlight specific features in the garden. It can be created through differences in color, texture, form, or size:

1. *Color Contrast*: To pull this one off, consider using complementary colors or perhaps a mix of warm and cool colors.

2. *Texture Contrast*: You may consider incorporating different textures (think rough stone paths with soft foliage, etc.).

3. *Form Contrast:* You may pair different plant shapes and forms. For example, you may pair tall, spiky plants with low, rounded ones.

- **Functionality**

A garden must be functional. More than anything, it should cater to the needs of those who use it. This involves careful planning of space and layout.

There are two main elements to consider:

1. *Zones:* Consider creating different areas for different activities. You could have a dining spot, a space for relaxing, a patch for growing vegetables, etc.

2. *Accessibility*: You should consider having your paths wide enough and surfaces stable enough for easy, unencumbered movement.

- **Sustainability**

Sustainable garden design focuses on creating environmentally friendly spaces that conserve resources and support local ecosystems.

There are three main aspects to consider:

1. *Native Plants*: Try using plants that are well-adapted to the local climate and soil conditions.

2. *Water Conservation*: Consider implementing efficient irrigation systems, rainwater harvesting, and use of drought-tolerant plants.

3. *Wildlife Habitat:* Consider designing your garden with wildlife in mind. This will help provide food and shelter for birds, insects, and other creatures.

By understanding and applying these elements/principles of garden design, you will be well on your way to creating a garden that is not only beautiful but also one that is functional and sustainable.

Up next, we explore types of garden styles.

Types of Garden Styles

Garden styles are really diverse, and they reflect a variety of *cultural*, *aesthetic*, and *functional* preferences. Regardless of what you have – a sprawling yard perhaps or a compact balcony – there is, indeed, a garden style that suits both your space and your personal taste.

Here are some of the most popular types of garden styles to consider:

1. Formal Gardens

Formal gardens are characterized by their *symmetry*, precise *geometric shapes*, and *meticulous maintenance*. They often feature neatly trimmed hedges, well-defined pathways, and carefully planned plantings.

Here are some examples you should consider:

✓ ***French Formal Gardens:***

Inspired by the grandeur of Versailles, these gardens feature *large lawns*, *straight paths*, and *elaborate parterres* (ornamental garden beds).

✓ ***Italian Renaissance Gardens:***

Italian renaissance garden

These gardens emphasize symmetry, order, and the integration of architecture and garden design. Oftentimes, they include *terraces, fountains, and sculptures.*

2. Informal Gardens

Informal gardens are more relaxed and naturalistic. They place considerable emphasis on creating a harmonious blend between both the garden and the surrounding landscape. They often feature *winding paths, irregular plant groupings*, and a *mix of textures and colors.*

Here are some examples you should consider:

✓ **Cottage Gardens:**

Cottage garden

Dense plantings of *flowers, herbs, and vegetables* mark these. They also often have an overgrown, romantic feel.

✓ **Woodland Gardens:**

Woodland garden

These are designed to mimic natural forests. These gardens typically use native plants and are often shaded. They also often feature *ferns, wildflowers, and meandering paths.*

3. Modern and Contemporary Gardens

Modern and contemporary gardens emphasize *clean lines, minimalism,* and the use of *modern materials* like steel, concrete, and glass. Plantings are often simple and restrained.

Here are some examples you should consider:

- ✓ **Minimalist Gardens**: These focus primarily on simplicity and tranquility. They often employ a limited color palette and few well-chosen plants.

- ✓ **Urban Gardens**: These gardens are designed for small spaces (such as balconies) and make efficient use of *vertical space, container gardening,* and *multifunctional furniture.*

4. Mediterranean Gardens

The coastal regions of Southern Europe quite heavily inspire Mediterranean gardens. They often feature drought-tolerant plants, terracotta pots, and either gravel or stone paths.

Here are some examples you should consider:

✓ ***Tuscan Gardens:***

Tuscan Garden

These incorporate such elements as *olive trees, lavender, and rustic stonework*. Oftentimes, they also feature outdoor dining areas.

✓ ***Spanish Gardens:***

The liberal use of *tiles, fountains, and bright colors* characterizes these. They place quite an emphasis on outdoor living spaces as well.

5. Japanese Gardens

Japanese gardens focus on creating serene, meditative spaces that reflect natural landscapes. They often include water features, rocks, and plants that are carefully pruned.

Here are some examples you should consider:

✓ ***Zen Gardens:***

Zen Garden

These dry gardens, also known as *karesansui,* use rocks and sand to represent water and islands. Their main purpose is to create a space for contemplation/meditation.

✓ **Tea Gardens:**

These gardens are designed to be viewed from a tea house and include stepping stones, lanterns, and water basins.

6. Tropical Gardens

Tropical gardens are lush and vibrant. They feature a variety of exotic plants with large leaves, bright flowers, and interesting textures. They thrive in warm, humid climates.

Here are some examples you should consider:

- ✓ **Balinese Gardens**: These gardens incorporate water features, statues, and a mix of tropical plants, like palms, orchids, and bamboo.

- ✓ **Rainforest Gardens**: These emulate rainforests' dense, multi-layered structure. They place emphasis on biodiversity and ecological balance.

7. Desert Gardens

Desert gardens are designed to thrive in arid climates, using drought-resistant plants and minimal water. They often feature gravel, rocks, and succulents.

Here are some examples you should consider:

✓ ***Southwestern Gardens:***

Southwestern Garden

Common in the southwestern United States, these gardens use native plants like cacti, agave, and yucca.

✓ ***Australian Outback Gardens:***

These incorporate native Australian plants (think eucalyptus, acacia, and grevillea.)

8. English Gardens

English gardens, or ***English landscape gardens,*** emphasize naturalistic plantings and sweeping lawns. They often include elements like lakes, trees, groves, and classical architecture.

Here are some examples you should consider:

✓ ***English Cottage Gardens:***

English Cottage Garden

These are informal and densely planted. They employ a healthy mix of flowers, herbs, and vegetables.

✓ **English Country Gardens:**

English Country Garden

These feature expansive lawns, herbaceous borders, and carefully placed trees and shrubs.

9. Edible Gardens

Edible gardens focus on growing food plants, including vegetables, fruits, herbs, and edible flowers. They can (and should) be both beautiful and functional.

Here are some examples you should consider:

- ✓ **Kitchen Gardens**: These are often laid out in a grid pattern. As the name suggests, they are close to the kitchen for easy access to fresh produce.

- ✓ **Permaculture Gardens**: These are designed based on ecological principles. The primary aim of these is to create a self-sustaining ecosystem.

10. Water Gardens

Water gardens center around water features such as ponds, streams, or fountains. They can (albeit not a must) include aquatic plants and fish.

Here are some examples you should consider:

- ✓ **Koi Ponds:** These feature colorful koi fish and aquatic plants. They often feature rock formations and waterfalls.

- ✓ **Bog Gardens:** These are designed for wet areas. As such, they use plants that thrive in moist soil.

11. Rock Gardens

Rock or alpine gardens use rocks and stones as the main structural element. The plants are designed to grow in the crevices.

Here are some examples you should consider:

- ✓ **Alpine Gardens**: These mimic the conditions of mountainous regions. As such, they use plants that thrive in rocky, well-drained soil.

- ✓ **Zen Rock Gardens:** These use rocks and gravel to create abstract representations of natural landscapes.

12. Wildlife Gardens

Wildlife gardens are designed to *attract* and *support* local wildlife (birds, insects, and small mammals.)

Here are some examples you should consider:

- ✓ **Butterfly Gardens**: These primarily use nectar-rich plants. These plants serve to attract butterflies and other pollinators.

- ✓ **Bird Gardens:** These heavily feature bird feeders, bird baths, and plants that provide bird food and shelter.

With the basics of garden design covered, the next chapter explores planning your garden.

Chapter 2: Planning Your Garden – A Step-by-Step Guide

This chapter will comprehensively cover how to plan your garden to build on Chapter 1. We will focus on three main aspects here: setting your goals, assessing your space, and considering your climate and soil. Understanding these elements is utterly crucial if you're going to create a garden that not only meets your needs but also thrives in its environment.

Let's get started.

Part I: Setting Your Goals

Setting goals is a crucial first step in planning a garden. Clearly defined goals will do two things for you: they'll guide your decisions and help create a cohesive, functional outdoor space.

Here are the key considerations and steps that you need to take when setting your goals for garden planning:

- **Identify Your Purpose**

The first step in setting your garden goals should be to identify what the primary purpose of your garden is. Different gardens, as you may have picked up from the contents of Chapter 1, serve different functions. Understanding what you want to achieve will influence all other aspects of your planning.

Here are some garden purposes to consider:

1. *Relaxation and Leisure*: If your primary goal is to create a space for relaxation, then you may want to consider such elements as comfortable seating, soothing water features (think soft water falls), and fragrant plants.

2. *Entertainment:* You may prioritize an outdoor dining area to entertain guests. You could also have a barbecue space, a fire pit, and open spaces for socializing.

3. *Food Production:* If growing your own food is important, you will be best served by creating a kitchen garden. You can grow vegetables, herbs, fruit trees, etc.

4. *Aesthetic Appeal*: For those of us who mainly want a visually stunning garden, the focus should be on plant variety, color schemes, and landscape design elements (sculptures, water features, etc.).

5. Wildlife Habitat: We also touched on this one in Chapter 1. If supporting local wildlife is a goal you hold dear, plan for native plants, bird feeders, and water sources to attract and sustain wildlife.

- **Consider Your Environment**

The second step is to consider your environment. Understanding your local environment is critical to setting both realistic and achievable garden goals.

Here are the primary factors to consider:

1. *Climate:* Your region's climate will dictate what types of plants can thrive. As such, you will need to research hardy plants that suit your local weather conditions.

2. *Soil Type*: Soil quality and type have a significant say in plant choices. Conduct a soil test to determine its pH and nutrient levels.

3. *Sunlight:* Observe the sunlight patterns in your garden. Some plants require full sun, while others thrive in partial shade or full shade. Do ample research so you know what and where to plant.

- **Budget and Resources**

Your third step is to factor in your budget and resources. You need to set a realistic budget for your garden project. It is important that you consider both the initial installation costs and ongoing maintenance expenses:

1. *Initial Costs*: Your initial costs should include plants, soil amendments, hardscaping materials (like stones, bricks, or wood), and garden tools.

2. *Maintenance Costs*: With these, you need to factor in the cost of water, fertilizers, pest control, and potential professional gardening services.

- **Time and Maintenance Commitment**

The fourth step is to factor in time and maintenance commitment. You need to be honest about the amount of time you can dedicate to maintaining your garden if your garden is going to be around for the long haul. Different garden styles and plants require varying levels of care.

Here are the factors to consider when setting goals for your garden design in regard to this:

1. *Low-Maintenance Gardens*: Choose drought-tolerant plants, native species, and automated irrigation systems if you prefer a garden that doesn't require much upkeep. If not, then you can be more liberal with your plant choices.

2. *High-Maintenance Gardens*: If you enjoy gardening as a hobby, you may want to choose more labor-intensive plants like annuals. Or, you could go for a specialized garden, like a rose garden or bonsai collection.

- **Personal Style and Preferences**

Finally, consider your personal style and preferences. Your garden should reflect your personal taste and style.

There are two main factors to consider:

1. *Design Aesthetic*: Whether you prefer a modern garden, a minimalist garden, or an English cottage garden, your design aesthetic will guide your plant and material choices.

2. *Favorite Plants*: Incorporate your favorite plants. They could be colorful flowers, aromatic herbs, exotic

specimens, etc. Just make sure that you factor in the environmental factors we've highlighted.

With the goals covered, let's now explore assessing your space.

Part II: Assessing Your Space

Assessing your space will ensure that your design is both practical and well-suited to the environment. Once you develop a solid understanding of the specific characteristics of your garden area, it will help you make informed decisions about plant selection, layout, and overall design.

Here are the key aspects to consider when assessing your garden space:

- **Understanding the Size and Shape of Your Space**

The size and shape of your garden should/will significantly influence its design. Therefore, be sure to consider the following:

1. *Measurements:* Make sure to measure the dimensions of your garden accurately. This will help massively in planning the layout and estimating the materials needed.

2. *Shape:* Identify the shape of your garden. It could be rectangular, square, circular, or irregular. This will affect the arrangement of plants and garden features.

- **Analyzing Sunlight and Shade Patterns**

Different plants require varying amounts of sunlight. As such, understanding the light conditions in your garden is crucial.

Consider:

1. *Sunlight Exposure:* Observe how sunlight moves across your garden throughout the day. Note the areas that receive full sun (6 or more hours of direct sunlight), partial sun (4-6 hours), partial shade (2-4 hours), and full shade (less than 2 hours). This will help you understand what to plant and where to plant it.

2. *Seasonal Changes:* Consider how sunlight patterns change with the seasons. Also, consider that trees, buildings, and other structures may cast different shadows at different times of the year as well.

- **Evaluating Soil Quality**

Healthy soil is the foundation of a successful garden. Here are the primary factors to consider here:

1. *Soil Type*: Determine your soil type—sandy, clay, loamy, or a mixture. Each type has different drainage and nutrient characteristics, all of which will have a say on what you can plant.

2. *Soil pH*: Test the pH level of your soil. This will help you know if it's acidic, neutral, or alkaline. Pro tip: most plants prefer ***a pH range of 6.0 to 7.5.***

3. *Nutrient Levels:* Conduct a soil test to identify the nutrient levels and any deficiencies that need amendments to address.

- **Assessing Drainage and Moisture Levels**

Proper drainage is essential to prevent waterlogging and root rot. Here are a couple of factors to consider:

1. *Drainage Test:* Perform a drainage test by digging a hole, filling it with water, and observing how long it takes to drain. Slow drainage typically indicates poor soil structure that may require amendment.

2. *Moisture Levels*: Identify areas that retain water and those that dry out quickly. This will help guide your plant selection based on water needs.

- **Understanding Climate and Microclimates**

The local climate and microclimates within your garden space will impact plant choices and garden design. Here are a couple of factors to consider:

1. *Local Climate:* Research the general climate of your region. Ensure you include the average temperatures, rainfall, frost dates, and wind patterns.

2. *Microclimates*: Identify microclimates within your garden. These are areas that have unique conditions due to factors like shade from buildings, windbreaks from trees, warmth from concrete surfaces, etc.

- **Identifying Existing Features**

Take stock of any existing features that will influence your garden design. Here are a couple of factors to consider:

1. *Structures*: Note the location of buildings, fences, patios, and pathways. These can provide shelter, shade, and support for climbing plants.

2. *Vegetation:* Identify existing trees, shrubs, and plants. Based on your design goals, decide which ones to keep, remove, or relocate.

3. *Utilities:* Be aware of underground utilities like water lines, electrical cables, and gas pipes to avoid damaging them during planting.

- **Considering Accessibility and Movement**

Planning for easy access and movement throughout your garden will be necessary. Here are a couple of factors to consider:

1. *Paths and Walkways:*

Garden path

Design paths wide enough for comfortable walking and easy access to different garden parts. Also, consider materials like gravel, stone, or wood chips.

2. *Entry Points:*

Ensure the garden has clear entry points. This will make it inviting and easy to navigate.

- **Accommodating Future Growth and Changes**

Finally, think long-term when planning your garden to accommodate future needs. Here are a couple of factors to consider:

1. *Plant Growth*: Consider the mature size of plants. This will help avoid overcrowding and ensure they have enough space to thrive.

2. *Future Projects*: Plan for potential future additions. These may include additional garden beds, structures, new plantings, etc. Your options are limitless.

Next up, we explore climate and soil considerations.

Part III: Climate and Soil Considerations

The final aspect of planning your garden is considering climate and soil. When planning your garden, understanding your area's climate and soil conditions is fundamental to your plants' success. Here's a comprehensive guide to considering climate and soil while planning your garden:

- **Climate Considerations**

Your region's climate will play a crucial role in determining which plants will thrive in your garden.

Here are the key aspects of climate to consider:

1. *Temperature:*

- ✓ *Average Temperatures*: Research your area's average high and low temperatures throughout the year. This information will help in selecting plants that can withstand (and thrive in) local temperature ranges.

- ✓ *Frost Dates:* Identify the average first and last frost dates. Frost-sensitive plants need to be planted after the last spring frost and harvested before the first autumn frost.

2. *Rainfall:*

- *Annual Precipitation:* Know the average annual rainfall and its distribution throughout the year. Some plants require consistent moisture. Others are drought-tolerant and, as such, prefer dry conditions.

- *Seasonal Rain Patterns:* Understand the seasonal variations in rainfall. This knowledge is essential for planning irrigation systems. It is also important to pick the appropriate plants for each season.

3. *Humidity:*

- *Humidity Levels:* Different plants have varying tolerance levels for humidity. High humidity can promote fungal diseases in some plants, while others may thrive in such conditions. Be clued in on the humidity levels in your area so you know what to plant.

- *Microclimates:* Recognize microclimates *within your garden.* In the context of humidity, these are where humidity levels might differ. Think of areas near water features or dense plantings, etc.

4. Wind:

- *Wind Patterns:* Consider the prevailing wind directions as well as intensity in your area. Strong winds can damage plants, desiccate foliage, and erode soil.

- *Windbreaks*: If the winds in your area are particularly strong, plan for windbreaks such as *hedges, fences, or walls*. These will help protect sensitive plants and create a more stable microclimate.

5. Sunlight:

- *Sunlight Exposure*: Observe how much sunlight different parts of your garden receive. We touched on this earlier in the first section of this chapter.

- *Seasonal Changes*: Take note of how sunlight exposure changes with the seasons. This is because it will affect plant growth and blooming periods.

- **Soil Considerations**

Soil quality is as important as climate in garden planning.

Here's what you need to know about soil:

1. Soil Texture:

Soil can be sandy, loamy, or clayey. Each type has different characteristics:

- ✓ *Sandy Soil:* Sandy soil drains quickly, is low in nutrients and warms up quickly in spring, but it doesn't hold water well.

- ✓ *Clay Soil:* Clay soil retains water well and is high in nutrients but can be heavy, compacted, and slow to drain.

- ✓ *Loamy Soil:* This is the ideal soil type. It is well-balanced, with good drainage and nutrient content.

- ✓ *Testing Texture:* Perform a simple soil texture test to tell which soil you're working with. Do this by moistening a handful of soil and feeling its grittiness or smoothness.

2. Soil pH:

- ✓ *pH Levels*: Soil pH ranges from acidic (below 7) to alkaline (above 7). As stated before, most plants prefer a pH between 6.0 and 7.5.

✓ *Testing pH:* Use a soil pH test kit or send a sample to a local extension service for analysis. If necessary, amend the soil so you can achieve the desired pH for your plants.

3. *Nutrient Content:*

✓ *Macronutrients:* Ensure your soil has adequate levels of nitrogen (N), phosphorus (P), and potassium (K). All three are essential for plant growth.

✓ *Micronutrients:* Trace elements like iron, manganese, and zinc are also important for plant growth. Performing soil tests or sending a sample for analysis can reveal deficiencies.

✓ *Organic Matter*: Add compost or organic matter to your soil. This will help improve soil fertility, structure, and microbial activity.

4. *Drainage:*

✓ *Drainage Capacity:* Good drainage is essential to prevent waterlogged roots. Waterlogging can lead to root rot. You can conduct a percolation test by digging a hole, filling it with water, and observing how quickly it drains.

✓ *Improving Drainage*: Amend heavy clay soil with organic matter or create raised beds to help enhance drainage. For sandy soils, adding organic matter will help improve water retention.

5. Soil Compaction:

Compaction reduces pore space. This directly affects water infiltration, as well as root growth. This is especially common in high-traffic areas. *Aerate the soil* by tilling or using a garden fork to alleviate compaction. *Adding organic matter* can also help improve the soil structure.

With planning your garden covered comprehensively, your next step is to create a garden layout. The next chapter explores this in a comprehensive fashion.

Chapter 3: Creating a Garden Layout

Building on the previous chapter, we will comprehensively look at how to create a garden layout in this one. We will be focusing on three key aspects: drawing a basic layout, zoning your garden, and designing pathways and structures. All three elements are essential for organizing your garden effectively and ensuring a harmonious and functional design.

Let's get started.

A) Drawing a Basic Layout

The first step in creating your garden layout is drawing a basic layout. It will provide you with a visual guide that will go a long way in organizing your thoughts, ensuring that you incorporate proper spacing, and allowing for efficient planning.

Here's a comprehensive guide on how to draw a basic garden layout:

- **Gathering Tools and Materials**

Before you start drawing, you need to gather the necessary tools and materials, which include:

✓ *Conventional/Traditional Tools:*

1) *Graph Paper*: This will help maintain scale and proportions.

2) *Ruler or Scale:* This will help you draw straight lines and measure distances accurately.

3) *Pencil and Eraser:* These will help in correcting mistakes easily.

4) *Colored Pencils or Markers*: These tools will help you differentiate various elements and add details.

✓ *Technological Options:*

To create a basic layout of your garden with minimal exertion, you can use the following AI and technological tools:

1) *Garden Design Apps*: Apps like [Garden Planner](#)[i] or [Home Designer](#)[ii] offer user-friendly interfaces to design garden layouts by dragging and dropping plants, furniture, and other elements.

2) *3D Modeling Software:* Tools like [SketchUp](#)[iii] allow for more detailed and customizable designs, providing a 3D view of your garden layout.

3) *AI-based Plant Identification Apps:* Apps such as PlantSnap[iv] or PictureThis[v] can help identify plants in your garden, making it easier to include them accurately in your design.

4) *Online Garden Planners*: Websites like SmartDraw[vi] provide online templates and tools to create a garden layout.

5) *Augmented Reality (AR) Tools:* Apps like ARki[vii] can overlay digital plants and structures onto your real-world garden space, giving a realistic preview of your design.

To use these tools, measure your garden space and enter the dimensions into a garden design app or online planner. Use 3D modeling software to refine the layout, and employ AI-based plant identification apps to catalog your current plants. Augmented Reality tools can then visualize how new plants and features will look in your garden. Finally, satellite imaging can provide a comprehensive overview, ensuring your design fits the landscape well. This process allows you to create a detailed and accurate garden layout with minimal physical effort.

- **Understanding Your Space**

Begin by assessing your garden space. We've already explored this, so there's no need to go into detail. Measure the length and width of your garden space, and **note down any irregularities in shape**. Also, **include existing structures** (think buildings, fences, trees, paths, and patios), and mark these on your layout so you know to work around them from the jump.

- **Creating a Scaled Drawing**

A scaled drawing ensures that all elements are proportionate and that they fit well within the space.

Therefore:

- ✓ *Choose a Scale:* Common scales are 1:10 or 1:20. This means that 1 cm on paper represents 10 or 20 cm in the actual garden.

- ✓ *Draw the Outline*: Using your scale, draw the outline of your garden on graph paper. Ensure that you mark your boundaries accurately.

- **Identifying Zones and Functions**

Next, you need to divide your garden into different zones based on their intended use:

✓ *Functional Zones:* Identify areas for specific functions (seating, dining, vegetable gardening, flower beds, children's play areas, etc.).

✓ *Transition Areas*: Plan paths and walkways that connect these zones. This will help ensure easy movement throughout the garden.

- **Incorporating Key Elements**

Add key elements to your layout, and consider their size and location.

These include:

✓ *Structures*: Mark the locations of structures such as sheds, greenhouses, pergolas, and arbors.

✓ *Paths and Walkways*: Draw paths and walkways. Also, do consider materials like gravel, stone, or paving.

✓ *Water Features:* If you plan on including water features such as ponds, fountains, or bird baths, ensure that you mark their positions.

- **Planning Plant Placement**

Plan where to place different plants, considering their light, water, and space requirements:

✓ *Sunlight and Shade*: Indicate areas that receive full, partial, or full sun. Then, choose your plants accordingly.

✓ *Height and Spread*: Consider the mature size of plants. With this in mind, place taller plants at the back of borders or in areas where they won't block sunlight for shorter plants.

✓ *Groupings:* Try to group plants with similar water and light needs together. This will help in efficient watering and maintenance.

- **Adding Details and Refining the Layout**

Add details to enhance both the functionality and aesthetics of your garden, such as:

✓ *Borders and Edging*: Define borders and edging for your garden beds. This can help maintain a neat appearance.

- ✓ *Seating Areas:* Mark the seating areas with details such as benches, chairs, or hammocks.

- ✓ *Lighting:* Plan for garden lighting and mark the locations of light fixtures. Do not forget to consider power sources as well.

- **Reviewing and Finalizing Your Layout**

Here, you review your layout to ensure it meets your needs and is practical.

As such:

- ✓ *Reassess Zones:* Check if the functional zones are well-placed and connected.

- ✓ *Plant Placements:* Verify that plants are positioned based on their growth requirements and that they won't overcrowd.

- ✓ *Accessibility:* Ensure all areas are easily accessible and that the paths are logically placed.

- **Creating a Master Plan**

Once you are satisfied with your basic layout, create a master plan that includes all the elements in detail.

These include:

- ✓ *Detailed Drawings:* Prepare detailed drawings for specific areas. Think vegetable gardens, flower beds, seating areas, etc.

- ✓ *Phasing Plan:* If you plan to implement your garden in phases, then you need to indicate which parts will be developed first and how subsequent phases will integrate.

With this covered, let us now move on to zoning your garden.

B) Zoning Your Garden

Garden zoning ***means creating distinct areas or "zones" within your garden***, ***each designed for a particular use or theme***. These zones can be based on *functions, plant types, or just purely aesthetics*. The goal here is to make the garden more user-friendly, efficient, and visually appealing.

Here's a comprehensive guide on how to zone your garden:

- **Assess Your Space**

Your first step is to assess your garden space thoroughly. Understand its *dimensions, shape, existing features*, and *environmental factors.* We've already covered this step, so there's no need to repeat the aspects and elements.

- **Identify Your Needs and Preferences**

Determine what you want to achieve with your garden. Different people have different needs and preferences. As such, you need to list down the functions you want your garden to serve. We've also touched on this one, so there's no need to reiterate the steps.

- **Designate Zones Based on Functions**

Next, assign specific areas of your garden to different functions based on your needs and the site assessment.

These areas can include:

✓ *Relaxation Zones:* Place seating areas where you can enjoy the best views and natural light.

✓ *Entertainment Zones*: Position dining areas close to the house for convenience. Also, ensure they are spacious enough for guests.

✓ *Play Areas*: Choose a safe, visible area for children's play zones. Ideally, they should be away from hazardous features.

- ✓ *Productive Zones*: Choose sunny spots with good soil for vegetable and herb patches.

- ✓ *Aesthetic Areas*: Place your flower beds and water features in prominent, visually appealing locations.

- ✓ *Utility Areas:* Locate your compost bins and sheds in less visible but easily accessible spots.

- **Incorporate Microclimates**

Next, recognize and utilize microclimates within your garden. This will help optimize plant growth and comfort.

The two main microclimates to consider are:

- ✓ *Warm Microclimates:* Use south-facing walls or areas that receive more sunlight for plants that require warmer conditions.

- ✓ *Cool Microclimates*: Use shaded areas or spots sheltered from wind for plants that prefer cooler temperatures.

- **Plan for Utilities and Infrastructure**

Finally, consider the practical aspects of your garden design. These include water supply, lighting, and storage:

- ✓ *Irrigation*: Plan for efficient irrigation systems. Make sure that all zones receive adequate water.

- ✓ *Lighting*: Install garden lighting to enhance safety and ambiance. This is especially needed in relaxation and entertainment zones.

- ✓ *Storage*: Designate areas for tool sheds, compost bins, and other storage needs.

Tips for Effective Garden Zoning

1) Balance Aesthetics and Functionality

While it's important for each zone to serve its intended purpose, you should strive for a harmonious overall design that's visually appealing at the end of the day.

Therefore, take into consideration:

- ✓ *Plant Selection:* Choose plants that complement each zone's function and aesthetic.

- ✓ *Materials and Finishes:* Use consistent materials and finishes to create a cohesive look.

2) Think Long-Term

Plan for future growth and changes in your garden, such as:

- ✓ *Plant Growth:* Consider the mature size of plants and how they will impact each zone.

- ✓ *Flexibility:* Design zones that can be easily adapted/expanded as your needs change.

3) Maintain Proportion and Scale

Ensure that each zone is appropriately scaled to fit the overall garden and its surroundings:

- ✓ *Proportional Spaces*: Avoid overcrowding. You can accomplish this by allocating adequate space for each zone.

- ✓ *Balanced Layout:* Distribute zones evenly to avoid an unbalanced look.

Next up, we explore designing pathways and structures.

C) Designing Pathways and Structures

Aptly designing your pathways and structures will help enhance *functionality*, *accessibility*, and *aesthetics*. Thoughtfully planned pathways guide movement and create flow, while structures like pergolas, arbors, and benches add architectural interest and practical use to the garden.

Here's a comprehensive guide to designing pathways and structures for your garden:

- **Designing Pathways**

Pathways in gardens amount to more than just functional elements; they also contribute to the garden's visual appeal. Well-designed pathways create a cohesive, inviting, and accessible garden space.

Here are the primary aspects and components to consider:

✓ *Purpose and Function*

Determine the primary purpose of each pathway in your garden:

1) *Primary Paths:* Refers to the main walkways connecting major areas like the house, garage, and patio. They should be wide, durable, and easily navigable.

2) *Secondary Paths:* Refers to the smaller paths that lead to specific garden areas, such as vegetable beds or flower gardens. These can be narrower and made of less formal materials.

3) *Decorative Paths*: These paths enhance the aesthetic appeal. Think of Winding Trails et al. These can be creative and whimsical in design.

✓ **Materials**

Choose materials that complement your garden's style and meet functional needs:

The common garden materials are:

1) *Gravel:*

Gravel path

This versatile, inexpensive option is suitable for informal and rustic gardens. It provides good drainage but may require regular maintenance.

2) *Pavers and Bricks*: These are durable, attractive, and especially ideal for formal gardens. They offer a wide range of colors, shapes, and patterns to work with.

3) *Stone:* Natural stone pathways blend well with most garden styles and offer a timeless and sturdy option.

4) *Wood:* Wooden pathways or stepping stones add a natural and warm touch. However, understand that they require regular upkeep to prevent rot.

5) *Concrete:* Durable and customizable, concrete can be stamped or stained to mimic other materials. It's suitable for modern and contemporary gardens.

✓ **Design and Layout**

Plan the layout to ensure smooth flow and visual appeal.

Here are the factors to consider:

1) *Width and Accessibility*: Primary paths should be at least 4 feet wide. This will help allow easy passage. Secondary

paths can be narrower but should still accommodate comfortable walking.

2) *Shape and Curvature*: Straight paths create a formal look, while curved paths add a sense of mystery and exploration. Ensure that your curves are gentle to maintain accessibility.

3) *Connectivity:* Connect key areas of the garden to help ensure "logical flow" and easy navigation. You can use focal points like statues or water features to guide the direction.

4) *Edging*: Define path edges with bricks, stones, or metal materials. This will help keep the pathway neat and prevent soil erosion.

✓ **Safety and Maintenance**

Lastly, ensure pathways are safe and easy to maintain by considering the following:

1) *Non-Slip Surfaces*: Choose materials that provide good traction. This will help prevent slips, especially in wet conditions.

2) *Level Ground:* Ensure paths are level and free of tripping hazards. For sloped areas, consider steps or terraces.

3) *Maintenance*: Select materials that require minimal upkeep. Also, regularly check for weeds, loose stones, or damaged sections and repair them as needed.

Up next, we explore designing structures.

- **Designing Structures**

Structures, such as pergolas, arbors, benches, and sheds, help add dimension, functionality, and beauty to the garden. They provide focal points, shade, seating, and storage, which enhance the overall garden experience.

Here are the main aspects to consider:

✓ *Types of Structures*

Incorporate various structures based on your garden's needs and style:

1) Pergolas and Arbors:

Arbor

These provide shade, define spaces and support climbing plants. **Pergolas are** larger and offer more coverage, while **arbors are** smaller and often serve as entryways.

Garden Designer for Beginners

2) Gazebos and Pavilions:

Gazebo

These offer sheltered seating areas and are ideal for relaxation and outdoor dining. They can even be focal points in larger gardens.

3) Sheds and Greenhouses:

These provide storage for tools, equipment, and plants. Greenhouses extend the growing season and allow for a wider variety of plants.

4) **Benches and Seating Areas:**

Sitting area

These create spots to sit and enjoy the garden. Place your benches in strategic locations to offer views of key areas.

5) **Fences and Trellises:**

These define boundaries, provide privacy, and support climbing plants. Trellises can be both decorative and functional.

✓ ***Material Selection***

Choose materials that match the garden's aesthetic and are durable, which can include:

1) *Wood*: Natural and versatile, wood can be used for a variety of structures. However, regular maintenance is required to help prevent weathering.

2) *Metal:* Strong and durable, metal structures can either have a modern or traditional look. They are low-maintenance but may need rust protection.

3) *Stone and Brick*: These are ideal for permanent structures. Think benches, walls, and pathways. They offer a classic, sturdy option.

4) *Vinyl and Composite*: These are low-maintenance alternatives to wood. They are available in various styles and colors.

✓ **Design and Placement**

Plan the design and placement of structures carefully to enhance functionality and aesthetics.

Here are the factors to keep in mind:

1) *Harmonize with the Garden*: Ensure your structures complement the garden's style and don't "overpower" the space.

2) *Strategic Placement*: Place your structures to create focal points, provide shade, and define spaces. Also, consider views from different angles.

3) *Scale and Proportion:* Make every effort to match the structure's size to the garden's scale. Also, avoid oversized structures that can dominate small spaces.

4) *Integration with Plantings*: Use plants to soften the edges of structures and blend them into the garden. Consider climbing plants on pergolas and arbors; they'll help create a cohesive look.

✓ **Functionality and Comfort**

Ensure structures serve their intended purpose and add to the garden's comfort:

1) *Shade and Shelter:* Provide adequate shade with pergolas, arbors, and gazebos. You may even consider retractable canopies or curtains for flexibility.

2) *Seating Comfort:* Choose comfortable seating options and place them in inviting locations. You can add cushions and pillows for extra comfort.

3) *Storage Solutions:* Design your sheds and storage areas to be functional yet unobtrusive. Follow up by organizing your tools and equipment efficiently.

Well-planned pathways ensure smooth movement and connectivity, while thoughtfully chosen structures add depth, interest, and practical use to the space. Next up, we explore incorporating functional elements in your garden.

Chapter 4: Incorporating Functional Elements in Your Garden

This chapter will comprehensively cover how to incorporate functional elements in your garden. We will explore three main components: seating areas and patios, water features, and garden lighting. These elements are essential for enhancing your garden's usability and aesthetic appeal.

Let's get started.

A) Seating Areas and Patios

Incorporating seating areas and patios into your garden design is essential for creating functional, inviting spaces that allow you to relax, entertain, and enjoy your little slice of outdoor heaven.

Here's a comprehensive guide on incorporating seating areas and patios into your garden:

- **Planning Your Seating Areas and Patios**

Here is how to go about this one:

✓ Assessing Your Needs

Before designing your seating areas and patios, it is important that you consider your specific needs and how you plan to use these spaces. You can always refer to our previous coverage since we've already gone in-depth on this one.

✓ Choosing the Right Location

Picking the optimal location for seating areas and patios is very important for comfort and convenience.

As such, consider the following:

1. *Proximity to the House*: If your primary objective for your garden is dining and entertaining, then a patio close to the kitchen will be proper and practical.

2. *Views and Privacy*: Place your seating where you can both enjoy the best views of the garden and maintain privacy.

3. *Sunlight and Shade*: Consider the sun's path to ensure that your seating area receives your desired amount of sunlight or shade.

4. *Shelter from Wind*: Choose a location that is sheltered from prevailing winds. This is because prevailing winds can be quite detrimental to comfort.

- **Designing Seating Areas**

✓ *Types of Seating*

Choose the type of seating that best suits your needs and garden style:

1. Benches:

These are versatile and can be placed in various locations. They are especially ideal for small gardens or as accents in larger spaces.

2. Chairs and Lounges:

Chairs in garden design

These provide individual comfort and can be moved around easily. They are ideal for relaxation and sunbathing.

3. Built-In Seating:

This option integrates very well with garden structures like retaining walls or planters. They also provide a permanent, cohesive look.

4. *Swing Seats and Hammocks:*

Hammock

These add a playful, relaxing element to your garden. However, they require sturdy supports or frames.

✓ **Materials**

Select materials that complement your garden's style and are durable for outdoor use, such as:

1. *Wood:* Wood offers a warm, natural look. However, regular maintenance is required to prevent weathering.

2. *Metal:* Metal is durable and can be crafted into intricate designs. But while it requires minimal maintenance, it may need rust protection.

3. *Stone*: Stone blends well with natural landscapes and is extremely durable. Most of the time, it is used for built-in seating.

4. *Wicker/Rattan*: This is lightweight and comfortable. It is quite suitable for covered or partially sheltered areas.

- ✓ **Placement and Design**

Plan the placement and design of seating areas to maximize comfort and aesthetics by considering the following factors:

1. *Focal Points:* Position your seating to face focal points (your water features, flower beds, views, etc.)

2. *Integration with Plantings:* Surround your seating areas with plants. This will help create a sense of enclosure and blend them into the garden.

3. *Comfort and Accessibility:* Ensure your seating is both comfortable and easily accessible from garden paths.

- **Designing Patios**

Here are the steps to follow:

✓ *Purpose and Functionality*

Patio chair

Outline the main purpose of the patio to guide its design:

1. *Dining and Entertaining*: This will require enough space for a dining table, chairs, and, possibly, a grill or outdoor kitchen.

2. *Relaxation*: This can include lounge chairs, a fire pit, or a water feature if you want a serene atmosphere.

3. *Multi-Use*: Try to design a flexible space that can accommodate an array of activities using modular furniture.

✓ **Materials and Surface Options**

Choose materials that suit your garden's style and meet functional requirements:

1. *Concrete*: This is versatile and durable and can be stamped or stained to mimic other materials. It is suitable if you are going for modern or contemporary designs.

2. *Natural Stone*: This offers an elegant, timeless look. It is available in various types like slate, flagstone, or bluestone.

3. *Brick*: Brick provides a classic, traditional appearance. It is durable and can be arranged in different patterns.

4. *Pavers*: Pavers are available in many shapes, colors, and materials. They are easy to install and replace if/when needed.

5. *Wood Decking:* Wood decking creates a warm, inviting surface. However, as you're clued in by now, regular maintenance is required to prevent decay and splintering.

✓ **Size and Layout**

Design your patio to accommodate the intended activities comfortably by doing the following:

1. *Scale*: Ensure the patio is proportionate to your garden and house size. Do your very best to avoid overwhelming small spaces or underutilizing large ones.

2. *Shape:* Choose a shape that complements the garden's design. You can go rectangular for formal gardens and irregular or circular for informal layouts.

3. *Zones:* Create distinct zones for different activities (dining, lounging, cooking, etc.).

- **Enhancing Seating Areas and Patios**

✓ **Shade and Shelter**

Provide shade and shelter to enhance comfort and usability by including some or any of the following:

1. *Umbrellas:* These are portable and adjustable and are suitable for flexible shading.

2. *Pergolas and Arbors*: These provide partial shade and support climbing plants. Chapter 6 will show you how to set these up.

3. *Awnings and Canopies:* These offer full coverage/protection from rain.

4. *Trees and Shrubs*: Consider getting natural shade from strategically planted trees and large shrubs.

✓ **Lighting**

Incorporate lighting to extend the use of seating areas and patios into the evening. The last section of this chapter comprehensively covers lighting and the array of options you have.

✓ **Accessories and Decorations**

Fire pit

Add accessories and decorations to enhance comfort and aesthetics, which can include:

1. *Cushions and Throws:* These will provide comfort and add color and texture.

2. *Planters and Containers:* These will help bring greenery and flowers close to your seating areas.

3. *Outdoor Rugs*: These will define your spaces and add a cozy feel to patios.

4. *Fire Pits and Heaters:* These will extend the usability of the patio into cooler months. (The image above is an example of a simple fire pit).

With this covered, let us explore how to set up water features.

B) Water Features

Incorporating water features into your garden design can (and will) inject a heavy dose of calm and tranquility and enhance its aesthetic appeal by a whole lot. Nothing helps bring a soothing atmosphere to a garden quite like water features do. Water features like ponds, fountains, waterfalls, and streams also add movement and sound to the garden.

Here's a comprehensive guide on including water features when incorporating functional elements in your garden:

- **Types of Water Features**

✓ *Ponds*

Ponds are versatile and can be designed to suit various garden styles and sizes:

1. *Formal Ponds*: These have geometric shapes and are often edged with stone or brick. They are suitable for structured gardens.

2. *Natural Ponds*: These have irregular shapes that blend seamlessly with the landscape. They mimic natural bodies of water.

3. *Wildlife Ponds*: These are designed to attract and support local wildlife. Oftentimes, they feature native plants and gentle slopes.

✓ *Fountains*

Fountains add elegance as well as a focal point to any garden.

You can have any of the following fountains:

1. *Standalone Fountains:*

Standalone Fountain

These can be placed anywhere in the garden. They are available in an array of styles, from classical to modern.

2. *Wall Fountains*: These are mounted on walls. They are ideal for small gardens or patios.

3. *Tiered Fountains*: These feature multiple levels from which water cascades. This setup creates a dynamic visual and auditory effect.

✓ *Waterfalls*

Waterfalls bring the sound of flowing water and a sense of movement:

Consider the following to incorporate a waterfall in your garden:

1. *Cascading Waterfalls*:

Cascading Waterfall

With these, water flows over a series of steps or rocks. This setup creates a gentle cascade.

2. *Sheet Waterfalls*: With these, water flows in a smooth, continuous sheet, offering a modern and sleek appearance.

3. *Pond-less Waterfalls*: With these, water recirculates without a standing body of water. These are safer for households with children or pets.

✓ **Streams and Brooks**

Streams and brooks add a natural, dynamic element to larger gardens:

1. *Meandering Streams*: These flow through the garden and create a sense of journey and exploration.
2. *Dry Streams*: These mimic the appearance of a streambed. However, they only carry water during rain and are often used in dry climates.

✓ **Reflecting Pools**

Reflecting pool

Reflecting pools create a serene and elegant effect, ideal for formal gardens. You can decide between either of these two:

1. *Still Water* Pools: These pools feature calm water reflecting the sky and surrounding plants. They have the effect of adding depth and tranquility.

2. *Infinity Pools:* These are designed to appear as though they merge with the horizon. They help add a modern, dramatic look to the garden.

- **Planning and Design Considerations**

✓ *Purpose and Aesthetics*

Define the purpose and desired aesthetic of your water feature, which could be:

1. *Relaxation*: Choose features that create a calming atmosphere (think gentle fountains and serene ponds.)

2. Entertainment: Opt for dynamic features (waterfalls and streams) that capture attention and provide a focal point.

3. *Wildlife Habitat*: Design with native plants and gentle slopes. This will help attract and support local wildlife.

✓ **Location**

Select the best location for your water feature based on several factors:

1. *Visibility:* Place water features where they can be easily seen and enjoyed and from various parts of the garden as well.

2. *Sunlight and Shade*: Consider the amount of sunlight the feature will receive. Too much sunlight can lead to algae growth in ponds, while too little can affect water plants.

3. *Proximity to Utilities:* Ensure easy access to water and electricity for pumps and lighting.

✓ **Scale and Proportion**

Match the scale of the water feature to the size of your garden:

1. *Small Gardens:* Choose compact features (wall fountains or small ponds) to avoid overwhelming the space.

2. *Large Gardens*: Incorporate larger features (expansive ponds, long streams, or multiple interconnected elements.)

- **Installation and Maintenance**

✓ *Installation*

Proper installation is crucial for the longevity and functionality of water features:

1. *Professional Installation:* Consider hiring professionals for complex features like ponds or large waterfalls. This will help ensure proper construction and integration with garden systems.

2. *DIY Projects*: Simpler features like small fountains or pond-less waterfalls can be DIY projects, at least if you have the necessary skills and tools.

✓ *Maintenance*

Regular maintenance keeps your water features in top condition.

Therefore, ensure the following factors are considered and met:

1. *Cleaning:* Regularly remove debris, clean surfaces, and prevent algae buildup.

2. *Water Quality:* Monitor and maintain water quality. You can use treatments, if necessary, to prevent issues like algae or mosquito breeding.

3. *Pump and Filter Care:* Ensure the pumps and filters are clean and functioning properly. These are essential for circulation and filtration.

4. Winter Care: Prepare water features for winter by draining them or using heaters to prevent freezing damage in colder climates.

- **Enhancing the Surroundings**

✓ *Plantings*

Incorporate plants that complement and enhance the water feature, such as:

1. *Aquatic Plants*:

Aquatic plants

Use water lilies, lotus, and other aquatic plants to add a dash of color and texture to ponds.

2. *Marginal Plants*: Plant reeds, rushes, and other moisture-loving plants around the edges of your water features.

3. *Surrounding Vegetation*: Select plants that thrive in the microclimate created by the water feature. For instance, you may consider ferns or hostas for shaded, moist areas.

✓ *Lighting*

Add lighting to extend the enjoyment of your water feature into the evening. The next section goes into ample detail on the subject of lighting.

✓ *Seating and Viewing Areas*

Create comfortable spots to sit and enjoy the water feature. We've already explored seating options in this chapter. Up next, we explore garden lighting.

C) Garden Lighting

Incorporating apt garden lighting into your outdoor space will significantly enhance its beauty, functionality, and safety. Thoughtfully designed lighting will also highlight key features and allow you to enjoy your garden long after the sun sets.

Here's a comprehensive guide on incorporating garden lighting:

- **Types of Garden Lighting**

✓ *Path Lighting*

Path lighting is essential for safety and navigation:

The main garden path lighting includes:

1. *Stake Lights*: These are placed along pathways. These lights illuminate walkways and prevent trips and falls.

2. *Recessed Lights:* These are installed into the ground or pathway surfaces, offering a sleek, unobtrusive look.

3. *Bollard Lights:*

Bollard lights

These are essentially short, vertical posts with light fixtures on top. They are great if you want widespread light.

✓ **_Spotlights and Floodlights_**

These lights are used to highlight specific features and provide broader illumination.

1. *Spotlights:* These focus a narrow beam of light on particular features (think statues, trees, architectural elements, et al.)

2. *Floodlights*: These provide broad, intense light. They are ideal for security or illuminating large areas.

✓ **_Ambient and Decorative Lighting_**

Enhance the mood and aesthetic of your garden with ambient and decorative lighting, like:

1. *String Lights:*

String lights

These are versatile and festive. They are perfect for patios, pergolas, and trees.

2. *Lanterns*:

These add a touch of charm and can be placed on tables, hung from hooks, or set along pathways.

3. *Fairy Lights*:

Fairy lights

Small, delicate lights create a whimsical atmosphere. They are ideal for smaller plants or decorations.

4. *Candles and Torches:*

These provide soft, flickering light. They are great for enhancing the romantic or tropical feel of the garden.

✓ **Underwater and Water Feature Lighting**

Enhance water features with the following specialized lighting:

1. *Submersible Lights*: These are placed inside ponds, fountains, or pools and illuminate the water from within.
2. *Floating Lights:* These are buoyant lights that drift on the surface of water features and create a magical effect.
3. *Waterfall Lights*: These are installed within or around waterfalls. They help highlight the cascading water.

✓ **Wall and Step Lighting**

Ensure safety and highlight vertical surfaces with wall and step lighting:

1. *Wall Lights:* These are mounted on garden walls or fences. They are great for general illumination or highlighting textures.

2. *Step Lights:* These are installed on steps or stairs. They help prevent accidents as well as enhance visibility.

- **Planning and Design Considerations**

✓ ***Purpose and Functionality***

Determine the primary purpose of your garden lighting to guide your design choices:

1. *Safety and Security:* Use path, flood, and step lights to ensure safe navigation and deter intruders.

2. *Aesthetics and Ambiance*: Opt for string lights, lanterns, and spotlights to create a warm, inviting atmosphere.

3. *Highlighting Features:* Use spotlights, underwater lights, and wall lights to draw attention to specific garden elements.

✓ ***Location and Placement***

Strategically place lights to maximize their effectiveness and visual appeal.

Here is how:

1. *Paths and Walkways*: Ensure all pathways are well-lit for safe movement.

2. *Focal Points:* Highlight trees, sculptures, water features, and other key elements.

3. *Seating and Dining Areas:* Provide sufficient light for garden activities while maintaining a cozy feel and vibe.

4. *Entrances and Exits*: Illuminate the doorways, gates, and entry points for security and convenience.

✓ **Lighting Techniques**

Utilize various lighting techniques to achieve desired effects:

1. *Up-lighting*: Place lights at ground level, pointing upward. This will help highlight structures or trees and create a dramatic effect.

2. *Downlighting:* Install lights above an area, casting light downward to simulate natural light and reduce glare.

3. *Backlighting*: Position lights behind objects so as to create silhouettes and depth.

4. *Grazing*: Place lights close to flat surfaces, like walls, to help accentuate textures.

- **Types of Light Sources**

✓ *LED Lights*

LEDs are energy-efficient, long-lasting, and versatile.

Benefits: They are low energy consumption, provide minimal heat output, and are available in various colors and intensities.

Uses: They are suitable for all types of garden lighting, from path lights to underwater lights.

✓ *Solar Lights*

These lights provide an eco-friendly option, and they are easy to set up.

Benefits: There's no need for wiring; they're powered by renewable energy and are cost-effective.

Uses: Ideal for path lights, stake lights, and decorative lighting.

✓ *Halogen Lights*

Halogen lights provide bright, intense light but consume more energy.

Benefits: They have excellent color rendering and brightness.

Uses: Common in spotlights and floodlights.

✓ *Low-Voltage Lights*

Low-voltage lights are safe and relatively easy to install.

Benefits: They are energy-efficient, safer for outdoor use, and provide good illumination.

Uses: They are suitable for a wide range of applications, including path lights, spotlights, and accent lights.

- **Installation and Maintenance**

✓ *Installation*

Proper installation ensures the safety and longevity of your garden lighting:

1. *Planning:* Map out your lighting plan and consider power sources and placement.

2. *Wiring*: For wired systems, ensure proper insulation and protection from moisture. Make use of waterproof connectors and cables.

3. *Mounting*: Secure your lights properly so as to help withstand weather conditions and prevent damage.

- ✓ **Maintenance**

Regular maintenance keeps your garden lighting in optimal condition:

1. *Cleaning*: Clean light fixtures regularly to remove dirt, dust, and debris.

2. *Bulb Replacement*: Check and replace burnt-out bulbs promptly.

3. *Checking Connections:* Inspect wiring and connections periodically for signs of wear or damage.

4. *Adjustments:* Adjust the positioning of lights as plants grow or as landscape features change.

- **Enhancing Garden Lighting**

- ✓ ***Integration with Landscape***

Blend lighting seamlessly into your garden design:

1. *Concealed Fixtures*: Hide light sources within plants or structures to create a natural look.

2. *Blending with Plants*: Use plant-friendly colors and designs that complement your garden's flora.

3. *Harmonizing Styles*: Ensure the lighting style matches your garden's overall theme (be it modern, rustic, traditional, etc.)

✓ **Smart Lighting Systems**

Incorporate smart technology for convenience and efficiency, such as:

1. *Sensors and Timers*: Automate lighting using motion sensors and timers. This will have the effect of saving energy and enhancing security.

2. *Remote Control*: Install systems that can be controlled via smartphone apps for easy adjustments.

3. *Dimmable Lights*: Choose dimmable lights to adjust brightness in accordance with mood and activity.

✓ **Eco-Friendly Options**

Opt for sustainable lighting solutions to reduce environmental impact:

1. *Solar-Powered Lights:* You may utilize solar energy to power your garden lights, reducing electricity usage.

2. *Energy-Efficient Bulbs:* Consider choosing LED or other energy-efficient bulbs for all fixtures.

3. *Recycled Materials*: Consider using fixtures made from recycled or sustainable materials.

With all this covered, the next chapter transitions to soil preparation and planting.

Chapter 5: Soil Preparation and Planting – A Comprehensive Guide

In this chapter, we will comprehensively cover soil preparation and planting. We will focus on three critical aspects: soil preparation and testing, planting techniques, and mulching and watering. These foundational steps are essential if you want healthy plant growth and a thriving garden.

Let's get started.

A) Soil Testing and Improvement

Preparing and testing the soil is a critical step when building your garden. Proper soil preparation will ensure that your plants receive the necessary nutrients, water, and aeration to grow healthy and strong.

Here's a comprehensive guide on the same:

- **Soil Preparation**

✓ *Clearing the Site*

Begin by clearing the area of any debris, weeds, and unwanted vegetation:

1. Clear away rocks, sticks, and other debris from the site.

2. Pull out weeds by hand or use a hoe. Consider using a weed killer for stubborn weeds, but ensure it's safe for future planting.

3. If there are existing plants that you do not want, remove them completely, *including the roots*.

✓ **_Loosening the Soil_**

Loosening the soil improves its structure and aeration, making it easier for roots to grow:

1. *Digging*: Use a shovel or garden fork to turn the soil to a depth of at least 12 inches. Break up large clumps to ensure the soil is loose and crumbly.

2. *Tilling*: For larger areas, use a rototiller to loosen the soil. Be cautious, however, not to over-till, as doing so can damage soil structure.

✓ **_Improving Soil Structure_**

Amending the soil enhances its physical properties, making it more suitable for plant growth:

1. *Compost*: Add a 2-4-inch layer of compost to the soil and mix it thoroughly. Compost improves soil structure, moisture retention, and nutrient content.

2. *Manure*: Well-rotted manure is another excellent organic amendment. It adds nutrients and improves soil texture.

3. *Organic Matter*: Incorporate other organic matter, such as leaf mold, peat moss, or aged sawdust.

✓ **Adjusting Soil pH**

Soil pH affects nutrient availability to plants. The vast majority of garden plants do best in a slightly-acidic-to-neutral pH (6-7), and to adjust it:

1. *Testing pH*: Use a soil pH test kit or send a soil sample to a local extension service to determine the pH level. We highlighted this earlier in the book.

2. *Raising pH (liming):* If the soil is too acidic, add lime (calcium carbonate). Apply according to the test results, and ensure it is mixed thoroughly.

3. *Lowering pH:* If the soil is too alkaline, add sulfur or peat moss to lower the pH. Again, do apply according to the test results.

✓ Fertilizing

Adding fertilizers provides essential nutrients that may be lacking in the soil:

1. *Balanced Fertilizers*: Use a balanced, slow-release fertilizer. This will help provide a steady supply of nutrients.

2. *Organic Fertilizers*: Consider using organic options (bone meal, blood meal, or fish emulsion) for a more sustainable approach.

3. *Application*: Follow the manufacturer's recommendations for application rates and methods.

- **Soil Testing**

✓ Collecting Soil Samples

Accurate soil testing begins with proper sample collection:

1. *Tools Needed:* Have a clean trowel, soil probe – or shovel – and a clean container.

2. Sampling Depth: Take samples from 6-8 inches deep for most gardens. For lawns, sample at 2-4 inches depth.

3. *Multiple Locations*: Collect soil from multiple locations in your garden (About 5-10 spots) to get a representative sample.

4. *Mixing Samples*: Combine the samples in the container and mix thoroughly to create a composite sample.

✓ **Conducting the Test**

There are several ways to test your soil, from DIY kits to professional lab services:

1. *Home Test Kits:* These are easily available at garden centers. These kits provide basic information on pH, nitrogen, phosphorus, and potassium levels.

2. *Professional Lab Testing*: Sending your composite sample to a professional lab will give you a comprehensive analysis of your soil, including micronutrients and organic matter content.

✓ **Interpreting Results**

Understanding your soil test results is crucial for making informed amendments:

1. *pH Levels:* Adjust as needed, using lime to raise pH or sulfur to lower pH. There's no need to delve deeper into this one, as we've already gone into detail.

2. *Nutrient Levels*: Identify deficiencies, or excesses, in primary nutrients (N, P, K) and micronutrients. Follow the recommendations for specific fertilizers or soil amendments.

3. *Organic Matter:* Aim for **at least 5% organic matter** for optimal soil health. Add compost or other organic materials, if necessary.

✓ ***Making Amendments Based on Test Results***

Apply soil amendments based on your soil test results to correct any deficiencies or imbalances:

1. *Nitrogen*: If low, use blood meal, fish emulsion, or a high-nitrogen fertilizer.

2. *Phosphorus:* If low, add bone meal, rock phosphate, or a high-phosphorus fertilizer.

3. *Potassium:* If low, use wood ash, kelp meal, or a high-potassium fertilizer.

4. *Micronutrients*: Apply specific amendments, as needed, for deficiencies in micronutrients like magnesium, calcium, or iron.

- **Maintaining Soil Health**

✓ ***Regular Testing***

Regular soil testing ensures your soil remains in optimal condition:

1. *Frequency:* Test your soil every 2-3 years or whenever you notice poor plant performance.
2. *Adjustments:* Make necessary adjustments based on test results to maintain soil health.

✓ ***Crop Rotation***

Rotating crops helps prevent nutrient depletion and reduces pest and disease buildup:

1. *Planning*: Plan your garden layout to avoid planting the same family of plants in the same spot year after year.
2. *Diverse Planting:* Include a variety of plant types in your rotation plan. This will help maintain soil fertility and structure.

✓ **Cover Crops**

Growing cover crops improves soil health during the off-season:

Benefits: Cover crops prevent erosion, add organic matter, and improve soil structure.

Types: Consider legumes (which fix nitrogen) and grasses, or just go with a mix of different plants.

With soil testing and preparation adequately covered, let us now explore planting techniques.

B) Planting Techniques

Planting techniques play a crucial role in the success of your garden. Proper planting will help ensure that your plants establish well, grow healthily, and thrive in your garden environment.

Here's a comprehensive guide on effective planting techniques:

- **Selecting the Right Plants**

✓ ***Consider Climate and Zone***

To do this:

1. *USDA Hardiness Zone:* Determine your garden's USDA Hardiness Zone[viii] to select plants that will thrive in your climate. The USDA hardiness zone system classifies geographic areas based on their average annual minimum winter temperatures. Each zone is defined by a 10-degree Fahrenheit range, with **Zone 1 being the coldest and Zone 13 the warmest.**

2. *Microclimates*: Consider microclimates within your garden that might affect plant growth.

✓ ***Plant Requirements***

1. *Light*: Choose plants based on the available sunlight—full sun, partial shade, or full shade.

2. *Soil*: Ensure the soil type (clay, loam, sandy) and pH match the plants' needs.

3. *Water*: Select plants with similar watering needs and group them together. This will help facilitate efficient irrigation.

- **Preparing the Planting Site**

✓ ***Soil Preparation***

1. *Clear the Area*: Remove rocks, weeds and any kind of debris from the planting area.

2. *Loosen Soil*: Use a shovel or garden fork to till the soil to a depth of 12-15 inches. This will help improve aeration and root penetration.

3. *Amend Soil*: Add compost or well-rotted manure to enrich the soil and improve its texture and fertility.

✓ ***Layout Planning***

1. *Spacing*: Plan for adequate spacing based on the mature size of the plants. This will help avoid overcrowding.

2. *Arrangement*: Arrange plants according to their height and spread, placing taller plants at the back and shorter ones at the front for visibility and sunlight access.

- **Planting Techniques**

✓ ***Seed Planting***

1. *Direct Sowing:*

Sow seeds directly into the garden bed if they are suited to direct sowing:

- Depth: Plant seeds at the recommended depth, usually 2-3 times their diameter.
- Spacing: Follow the spacing guidelines on the seed packet to prevent overcrowding.
- Watering: Water gently but thoroughly to keep the soil moist until seeds germinate.

2. *Indoor Starting:*

Start your seeds indoors if they need a longer growing season:

- Containers: Use seed trays or small pots with a seed-starting mix.
- Light: Provide sufficient light using grow lights or a sunny window.

> Transplanting: Transplant seedlings to the garden when they have true leaves and when the risk of frost has passed.

✓ ***Transplanting Seedlings***

To do this:

1. *Harden Off*: Slowly but steadily acclimate your seedlings to the outdoors. You do this by gradually exposing them to greater sunlight and outdoor temps over 7-10 days.

2. *Planting Holes*: Dig holes slightly bigger than the seedling root balls.

3. *Placement:* Place the seedling in the hole at the same depth that it was growing in the pot.

4. *Backfill:* Add back soil into the hole and gently firm it around the base of the plant.

5. *Watering*: Make sure to water adequately (meaning thoroughly) after you plant to settle the soil around the roots.

✓ *Planting Container Plants*

Here are the steps to follow:

1. *Watering*: Water the plants in their containers before planting.

2. Planting Hole: Dig a hole twice as wide and as deep as the root ball.

3. *Root Pruning*: If the plant is root-bound, lightly tease the roots apart or make a few vertical cuts. This will help encourage outward growth.

4. *Plant Placement*: Position the plant in the hole so that the top of the root ball is level with the soil surface.

5. *Backfill and Firm*: Backfill with soil and firm it gently around the plant. This will help eliminate air pockets.

6. *Mulching*: Apply a 2-3-inch layer of mulch around the base of the plant, keeping it away from the stem to retain moisture and suppress weeds.

7. *Watering*: Water thoroughly to help establish the plant.

✓ *Planting Trees and Shrubs*

For trees and shrubs:

1. *Site Selection:*

- Space and Sunlight: Ensure adequate space for the mature size of the tree or shrub and appropriate sunlight conditions.

- Soil Drainage: Choose a site with good drainage to prevent waterlogging.

2. *Planting Procedure:*

- Hole Preparation: Dig a hole 2-3 times wider than the root ball and the same depth as the root ball.

- Root Inspection: Check the roots and prune any damaged or circling roots.

- Positioning: Place the tree or shrub in the hole, with the top of the root ball level with, or slightly above, the surrounding soil.

- Backfill: Fill the hole with the native soil, mixing in compost if needed. Firm the soil gently as you fill.

- Staking: Stake the tree, if necessary, to support it while it is established. Remove the stakes after the first growing season.

- Watering: Water deeply to ensure the root ball is saturated. Continue regular watering until the plant is well-established.

- Mulching: Apply a layer of mulch around the base, avoiding direct contact with the trunk.

With planting techniques adequately covered, let us now explore mulching and watering.

C) Mulching and Watering

Mulching and watering significantly contribute to plant health, soil fertility, and water conservation. Proper techniques in these areas can (and will) help create a thriving, sustainable garden.

Here's a comprehensive guide on effective mulching and watering:

- **Mulching**

Mulching involves **covering the soil with organic or inorganic materials**. This enhances soil conditions, conserves moisture, and suppresses weeds.

Here's how to do it effectively:

✓ **Choosing the Right Mulch**

1. *Organic Mulch*

Types: The main types include wood chips, bark, straw, grass clippings, compost, leaves, and pine needles.

Benefits: It improves soil structure, adds nutrients as it decomposes, and supports beneficial microorganisms.

2. *Inorganic Mulch*

Types: Gravel, pebbles, landscape fabric, plastic sheeting.

Benefits: It is long-lasting, good for pathways and areas where you don't want plant growth, and is effective at weed suppression.

✓ Preparing the Area

1. *Weed Removal*: Remove existing weeds to prevent them from growing through the mulch.

2. *Soil Cultivation*: Loosen the soil surface with a garden fork or hoe to improve aeration and water penetration.

✓ Applying Mulch

1. *Layer Thickness*: Apply a 2-4-inch layer of organic mulch. For inorganic mulch, 1-2 inches should be sufficient.

2. *Coverage:* Spread the mulch evenly around plants, and make sure not to pile it against plant stems or trunks. This will help prevent rot and disease.

3. *Edging:* Create a clear edge between mulched areas and lawns or pathways. This will help to both contain the mulch and maintain a tidy appearance.

✓ Maintaining Mulch

1. *Replenishment*: Add new mulch as needed to maintain the desired thickness. Do this once or twice a year for organic mulch.

2. *Weed Control*: Regularly check for and remove any weeds that penetrate the mulch layer.

3. *Aeration*: Occasionally, fluff up the mulch with a rake. This will help prevent compaction and maintain good air and water flow.

- **Watering**

Proper watering practices are essential to ensure plants consistently receive the ideal moisture for optimal growth.

Here's a detailed procedure for effective garden watering:

✓ ***Understanding Plant Water Needs***

1. *Know Your Plants:* Different plants have varying water requirements. As such, you need to group plants with similar needs to optimize watering.

2. *Type of Soil*: Sandy soils drain quickly and need more regular watering. Clay soils, on the other hand, maintain water for longer and require less regular watering.

3. *Climate and Season*: Adjust your watering frequency and amount based on seasonal changes and local climate conditions.

✓ Watering Techniques

1. Hand Watering:

Hand watering

- ➤ Tools: Use a watering can or hose with a soft spray nozzle.

- ➤ Method: Use your hand/s to water at the base of plants to ensure minimum water loss and reduce the risk of fungal diseases. Also, avoid wetting the foliage.

- ➤ Timing: Water your plants early in the morning or late in the afternoon. This will help reduce evaporation and allow your plants to absorb moisture before the heat of the day.

2. **Drip Irrigation:**

Drip irrigation

- ➢ Setup: Install a drip irrigation system with emitters placed near the base of plants.

- ➢ Benefits: It directly provides slow, consistent moisture to the root zone, conserving water and reducing evaporation.

- ➢ Maintenance: Regularly check for clogs and ensure emitters are functioning properly.

3. **Soaker Hoses:**

- ➢ Installation: Lay soaker hoses on the soil surface around plants and cover with mulch to distribute water evenly.

- ➤ Advantages: Efficiently helps water plants at the root level, minimizing water waste and evaporation.
- ➤ Use: Turn on the soaker hose for a set period. This will help ensure deep watering.

4. *Overhead Sprinklers:*

- ➤ Usage: These are suitable for larger areas like lawns or vegetable gardens.
- ➤ Considerations: They can lead to water waste via evaporation and runoff. Adjust the sprinkler heads to avoid over-saturating or missing areas.
- ➤ Timing: Water early in the morning to help reduce evaporation and fungal disease risk.

✓ **Watering Frequency and Amount**

1. *Deep Watering*: Water deeply but infrequently to encourage deep root growth. The soil should be moist to a depth of 6-8 inches.

2. *Check Soil Moisture*: Use a soil moisture meter or check by hand to determine if watering is needed. The top inch of the soil should be dry before watering again.

3. *Seasonal Adjustments*: Increase watering during hot, dry periods and reduce during cooler, wet seasons.

Proper watering techniques, including understanding plant needs, using appropriate watering methods, and conserving water, will help ensure that your plants receive adequate moisture for optimal growth.

Chapter 6: Constructing Garden Features – A Comprehensive Guide

In this chapter, we will comprehensively cover constructing garden features. We will explore three main components: building raised beds, installing pathways, and setting up pergolas and arbors. These structural elements are crucial, as they will help enhance your garden's functionality and visual appeal.

Let's get to it.

A) Building Raised Beds

Raised beds

Building raised beds is a practical and efficient way to create a productive and manageable garden. Here's a comprehensive guide on how to build raised beds:

Benefits of Raised Beds

1. *Improved Soil Quality*: Allows for customized soil mixtures.

2. *Better Drainage*: Reduces waterlogging, which is especially useful in areas with heavy rainfall.

3. *Weed and Pest Control*: Easier to manage and control.

4. *Ease of Access*: It is ideal if you have mobility issues, as it reduces the need for bending.

5. *Extended Growing Season*: Soil warms up faster in spring and retains heat longer in fall.

Materials Needed

1. *Lumber*: Cedar, redwood, or untreated pine are best for longevity and safety.

2. *Fasteners:* Use galvanized screws or nails to prevent rust.

3. *Tools*: You will need a saw, drill, measuring tape, level, shovel, and garden rake.

4. *Soil and Compost*: High-quality garden soil and compost.

5. *Weed Barrier*: Landscape fabric or cardboard to suppress weeds.

Step-by-Step Procedure

✓ ***Planning and Design***

1. *Size and Shape*: Standard beds are 4 feet wide to allow easy access from all sides and 6-8 feet long. Height can vary, but typically, 10-12 inches should suffice.

2. *Location*: Choose a sunny location with good drainage. Ensure that there is proximity to a water source and ease of access.

3. *Number of Beds*: Plan according to your gardening needs and available space.

✓ ***Selecting Materials***

1. *Lumber:* Choose rot-resistant wood, like cedar or redwood. Untreated pine is more affordable, but it may not last as long.

2. *Fasteners*: Use galvanized or stainless-steel screws or nails to prevent rusting.

✓ Building the Beds

1. *Cutting Lumber*: Measure and then cut the lumber to the desired lengths using a saw. For a 4x8 foot bed, cut two 4-foot pieces and two 8-foot pieces.

2. *Assembly:* Assemble the bed frame by attaching the side boards to the end boards. You can use screws or nails for this. Ensure that the corners are square using a carpenter's square.

3. *Reinforcements:* Add center supports to prevent bowing for longer beds. This is particularly important for beds longer than 8 feet.

✓ Preparing the Site

1. *Clearing*: Remove weeds, grass, and debris from the area where the bed will be placed.

2. *Leveling*: Level the ground using a shovel and rake to ensure the bed sits evenly.

3. *Weed Barrier*: Lay down landscape fabric or cardboard to suppress weeds. This will also help prevent grass and weeds from growing into the bed from below.

✓ Positioning the Bed

1. *Placement:* Place the assembled bed frame in the prepared location.

2. *Leveling:* Use a level to ensure the bed is even. Adjust the ground as needed to make sure the bed sits flat and stable.

✓ Filling the Bed

1. *Soil Mix*: Fill the bed with a mix of high-quality garden soil and compost. A common ratio is 60% topsoil, 30% compost, and 10% potting soil or other organic matter.

2. *Layering:* For deeper beds, consider layering with coarse organic material (like straw or wood chips) at the bottom for better drainage, topped with the soil mix.

✓ Planting

1. *Planning*: Plan your planting layout based on your plants' mature size and spacing requirements.

2. *Planting:* Plant seeds or seedlings according to the garden plan, ensuring adequate spacing for each plant to grow.

✓ Maintenance Tips

1. *Watering*: Regularly water the raised bed to moisten the soil, but not waterlogged. Raised beds can dry out faster than ground-level gardens, so monitor soil moisture closely.

2. *Weeding*: Mulch the surface to help retain moisture and suppress weeds. Remove any weeds that do appear promptly.

3. *Feeding*: Add compost or organic fertilizers to replenish nutrients, especially if you're growing heavy feeders like tomatoes or squash.

4. *Seasonal Care:* In colder climates, consider covering the beds with plastic or row covers to extend the growing season and protect plants from frost.

With this covered, let us now explore installing pathways.

B) Installing Pathways

Garden Pathway

Installing pathways in your garden enhances its aesthetic appeal and provides functional routes for easy access to different areas. Properly designed and constructed pathways will define your garden space, improve navigation, and reduce soil compaction in planting areas.

Here's a comprehensive guide on how to go about it:

Materials Needed

1. *Surface Materials*: Pavers, bricks, gravel, wood chips, or stepping stones.

2. *Edging Materials*: Brick, stone, metal, or plastic edging to contain the pathway surface

3. *Base Materials*: Crushed stone or gravel is used for the foundation.

4. *Weed Barrier*: Landscape fabric to prevent weed growth.

5. *Tools*: You will need a shovel, rake, tamper, level, measuring tape, wheelbarrow, and garden hose or string for layout.

Step-by-Step Procedure

✓ *Planning and Design*

1. *Pathway Route*: Decide on the route of the pathway. Use a garden hose or string to lay out the path and visualize its shape.

2. *Width and Shape*: Standard pathways are usually 2-4 feet wide. Consider wider paths for areas if you think there'll be quite a bit more foot traffic.

3. *Materials:* Choose pathway materials that complement your garden style and meet functional needs.

✓ Preparing the Site

1. *Marking the Path*: Mark the pathway edges using stakes, string, or a garden hose.

2. *Clearing*: Remove grass, weeds, and debris along the pathway route.

3. *Excavation*: Dig out the path to a depth of 4-6 inches, depending on the materials used and the level of traffic the pathway will endure.

✓ Installing the Base

1. *Weed Barrier*: Lay down landscape fabric. This will help prevent weed growth.

2. *Base Layer*: Add a 2-3-inch layer of crushed stone or gravel. This layer provides stability and drainage.

3. *Leveling*: Use a rake to spread the base material evenly, then tamp it down to create a firm foundation.

✓ Adding Edging

Purpose: Edging holds the pathway material in place and gives the path a finished look.

Installation: Install the chosen edging material along the sides of the pathway, ensuring it is level and securely anchored.

✓ ***Laying the Surface Material***

Depending on the type of surface material chosen, follow these specific steps:

1. *Pavers or Bricks:*

➤ Sand Layer: Spread a 1-2-inch layer of sand over the base material and level it.

➤ Laying Pavers/Bricks: Lay the pavers or bricks on the sand, fitting them tightly together. Use a rubber mallet to tap them into place.

➤ Leveling: Check the level frequently to ensure a flat surface.

➤ Finishing: Spread sand over the top and sweep it into the joints to lock the pavers in place. Follow up by wetting the surface to settle the sand and repeat as necessary.

2. *Gravel:*

➢ Gravel Layer: Spread a 2-3-inch layer of gravel over the base material.

➢ Raking: Use a rake to distribute the gravel evenly.

➢ Tamping: Lightly tamp the gravel to create a stable surface.

3. *Wood Chips:*

➢ Wood Chip Layer: Spread a 3-4-inch layer of wood chips over the base material.

➢ Evening Out: Use a rake to distribute the wood chips evenly.

4. *Stepping Stones:*

➢ Placement*:* Arrange the stepping stones on the base material, ensuring even spacing for comfortable walking.

➢ Stability*:* Add sand or soil under each stone to ensure they are stable and level.

➢ Filling Gaps: Fill gaps between stones with gravel, soil, or low-growing ground cover plants.

✓ Finishing Touches

1. *Cleanup*: Remove any excess materials and tools from the pathway area.

2. *Inspection*: Walk on the pathway to ensure stability and make any necessary adjustments.

3. *Maintenance*: Regularly check the pathway for any settling or shifting and replenish materials as needed.

Maintenance Tips

- ✓ **Regular Cleaning**: Sweep or hose down pathways to keep them clean.

- ✓ **Weed Control**: Remove any weeds that appear along the edges or between pathway materials.

- ✓ **Repairs:** Promptly repair any loose pavers, replenish gravel or wood chips, and fix edging as needed.

With this covered, let us now explore setting up garden structures.

C) Setting Up Garden Structures (Pergolas, Arbors)

Arbor

Setting up pergolas and arbors in your garden will enhance its aesthetic appeal, provide shade, and create a focal point, or gateway, that will add structure and interest.

Here's a comprehensive guide on setting up pergolas and arbors:

Materials Needed

1. *Lumber*: Pressure-treated wood, cedar, redwood, or vinyl.

2. *Fasteners*: You will need galvanized screws, bolts, or brackets.

3. *Concrete*: (For securing posts in the ground.)

4. *Tools*: Tape measure, level, post hole digger, shovel, saw, drill, ladder, and wheelbarrow.

5. *Plants*: Climbing plants, if desired; We would (and already have) recommend them.

Step-by-Step Procedure for Setting Up Pergolas

✓ *Planning and Design*

1. *Location:* Choose a location that complements your garden layout. Consider sunlight, proximity to other structures, and views, among other things.

2. *Size and Style*: Determine the size and style of the pergola. Ensure it fits the scale of your garden and the intended use.

3. *Permits*: Check with local authorities to see if permits are required.

✓ Materials and Tools

1. *Lumber*: Select rot-resistant wood such as cedar or redwood, or opt for vinyl for low maintenance.

2. *Fasteners*: Use galvanized or stainless-steel screws and bolts to prevent rusting.

3. *Concrete*: Use ready-mix concrete to secure the posts.

✓ Preparing the Site

1. *Marking the Area*: Use stakes and string to mark the location of the pergola posts.

2. *Clearing*: Clear the area of grass, weeds, and debris.

3. *Leveling*: Ensure the ground is where the posts will be placed level.

✓ Installing the Posts

1. *Post Holes*: Dig post holes at least 24-36 inches deep and 12 inches wide for stability.

2. *Positioning Posts:* Place a post in each hole, ensuring that they are level and plumb.

3. *Securing Posts*: Fill the holes with concrete around the posts and allow it to cure for 24-48 hours.

✓ **Building the Pergola Frame**

1. *Top Beams*: Attach the main beams (crossbeams) to the tops of the posts using bolts or brackets. Also, ensure that they are level.

2. *Rafters*: Install the rafters perpendicular to the main beams and ensure they're evenly spaced. Secure them with screws or brackets.

3. *Additional Supports*: Add any additional braces or supports as needed for stability.

✓ **Finishing Touches**

1. *Sanding and Staining*: Sand the wood to remove any rough edges. Stain or paint the pergola, both for protection and aesthetic appeal.

2. *Planting:* Plant climbing vines or other plants around the base of the pergola. This will create a lush, green canopy over time.

Step-by-Step Procedure for Setting Up Arbors

✓ Planning and Design

1. *Location:* Choose a spot that serves as an entryway or focal point. Common places include garden entrances, pathways, or transitions between garden areas.

2. *Size and Style*: Determine the size and style of the arbor to match your garden's aesthetics and function.

3. *Permits*: Check local building codes to see if permits are necessary.

✓ Materials and Tools

1. *Lumber*: Use durable wood, e.g., cedar or redwood, metal, or vinyl.

2. *Fasteners*: Galvanized screws, bolts, or brackets

3. *Concrete*: (This is for securing posts if necessary.)

✓ Preparing the Site

1. *Marking the Area:* Use stakes and string to outline the arbor's footprint.

2. *Clearing:* Clear the area of grass, weeds, and debris.

3. *Leveling*: Ensure the ground is level, where the posts will be placed.

✓ **Installing the Posts**

1. *Post Holes*: Dig post holes at least 18-24 inches deep for stability.

2. *Positioning Posts*: Place a post in each hole, ensuring they are level and plumb.

3. *Securing Posts:* Fill the holes with concrete around the posts if needed, and allow it to cure.

✓ **Building the Arbor Frame**

1. *Top Beams*: Attach the top beams to the posts using screws or bolts. Ensure they are level.

2. *Arched or Flat Top*: Install curved or straight top pieces depending on the design.

3. *Additional Supports*: Add lattice or braces to support and provide climbing surfaces for plants.

✓ Finishing Touches

1. *Sanding and Staining*: Sand the wood to smooth any rough edges. Stain or paint the arbor for protection and aesthetic enhancement.

2. *Planting*: Plant climbing vines or other decorative plants around the base of the arbor. This will enhance its appearance over time.

Maintenance Tips

- ✓ ***Regular Inspection***: Regularly check for loose fasteners and signs of rot or damage. Tighten and repair as needed.

- ✓ ***Cleaning***: Clean the pergola or arbor *annually* to remove dirt, mildew, and algae.

- ✓ ***Staining or Painting***: Re-stain or paint every few years to maintain the wood's protection and appearance.

- ✓ ***Plant Care:*** Prune climbing plants regularly to prevent overgrowth and ensure healthy growth.

Setting up pergolas and arbors will transform your garden into a stunningly beautiful yet awesomely functional space, and regular maintenance will ensure that your structures remain in excellent condition, bolstering your garden's beauty for years to come.

Conclusion

In conclusion, garden design should be an enriching experience that will help foster creativity, connection with nature, and a sense of accomplishment. By understanding and incorporating the fundamental principles of garden design, selecting appropriate plants, and learning basic maintenance techniques – all elements that we've covered comprehensively in this book – nothing will stop you from building a beautiful, sustainable garden.

With all this said, the world of garden design is vast and ever-evolving. For you to continue growing your skills and knowledge, it will be necessary to seek out additional resources, such as books, online courses, gardening clubs, local workshops, etc. Also, consider engaging with a community of fellow gardening enthusiasts and professionals, as this will help provide valuable insights and inspiration. Lastly, the best gardens are cultivated with curiosity and *a willingness to learn*. Keep this in mind.

Happy gardening!

PS: I'd like your feedback. If you are happy with this book, please leave a review on Amazon.

Please leave a review for this book on Amazon by visiting the page below:

https://amzn.to/2VMR5qr

Reference

i https://my-garden.gardena.com/int
ii https://www.homedesignersoftware.com/
iii https://www.sketchup.com/en
iv https://www.plantsnap.com/
v https://www.picturethisai.com/
vi https://www.smartdraw.com/
vii https://www.darfdesign.com/arki.html
viii https://planthardiness.ars.usda.gov/

Printed in Great Britain
by Amazon